I0825478

WELCOME TO
AFGHANISTAN
COUNTRIES OF THE WORLD
Afghanistan
by Bryan Langdo
BLASTOFF! READERS
2
BLASTOFF! READERS, AN IMPRINT OF BELLWETHER MEDIA BY FLUTTERBEE

Blastoff! Readers are carefully developed by literacy experts to build reading stamina and move students toward fluency by combining standards-based content with developmentally appropriate text.

LEVELS

Level 1 provides the most support through repetition of high-frequency words, light text, predictable sentence patterns, and strong visual support.

Level 2 offers early readers a bit more challenge through varied sentences, increased text load, and text-supportive special features.

Level 3 advances early-fluent readers toward fluency through increased text load, less reliance on photos, advancing concepts, longer sentences, and more complex special features.

★ **Blastoff! Universe**

Reading Level

Grade K

Grades 1–3

Grade 4

This edition first published in 2026 by Bellwether Media, Inc.

Library of Congress Cataloging-in-Publication Data is available at www.loc.gov or upon request from the publisher.

ISBN: 9798893047806 (hardcover)
ISBN: 9798893048803 (ebook)

Editor: Rachael Barnes   Designer: Brittany McIntosh

Printed in the United States of America, North Mankato, MN.

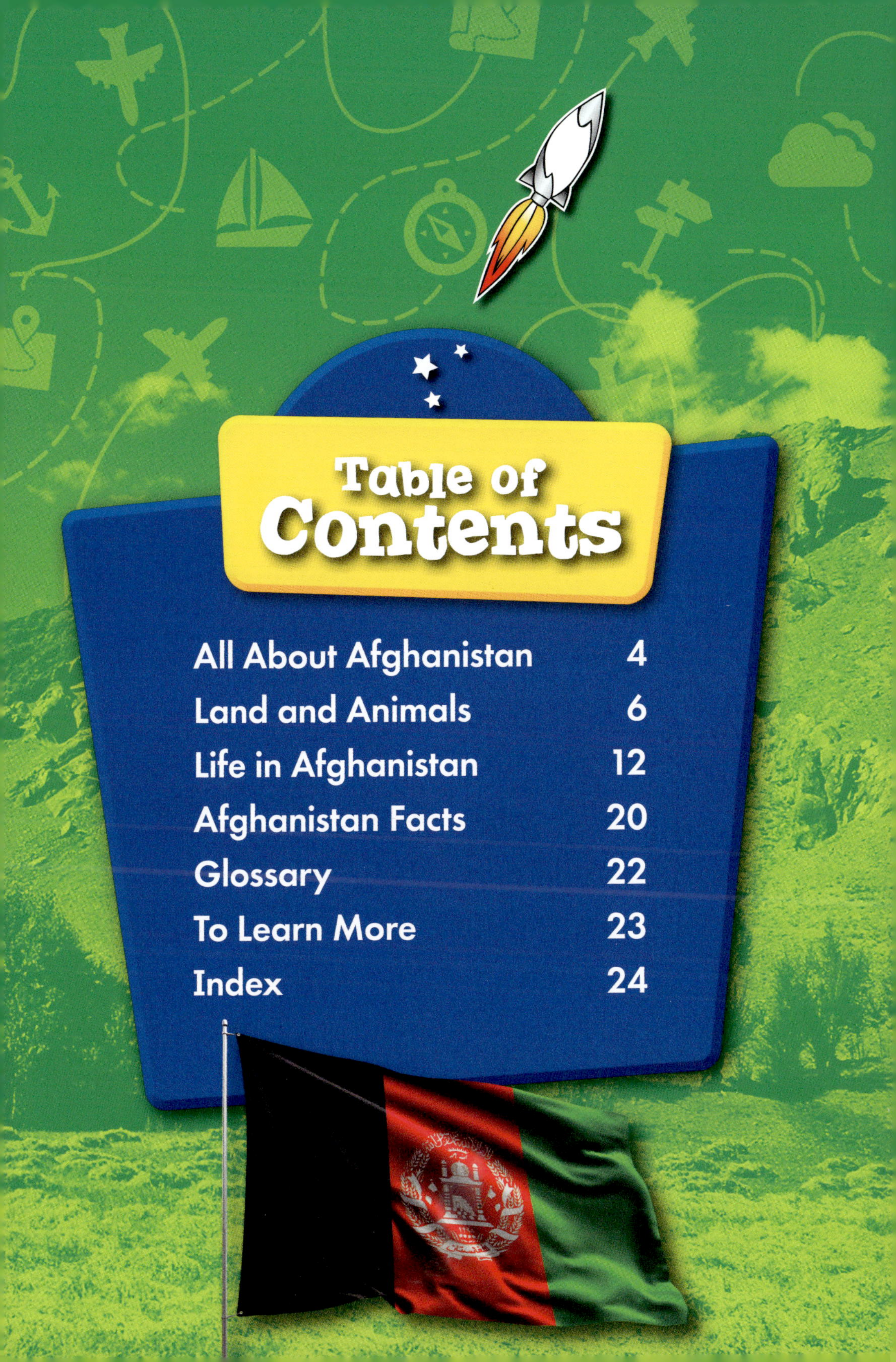

Table of Contents

All About Afghanistan

Kabul

Afghanistan is a **landlocked** country in Asia. Its capital is Kabul.

The country is sometimes called the "heart of Asia."

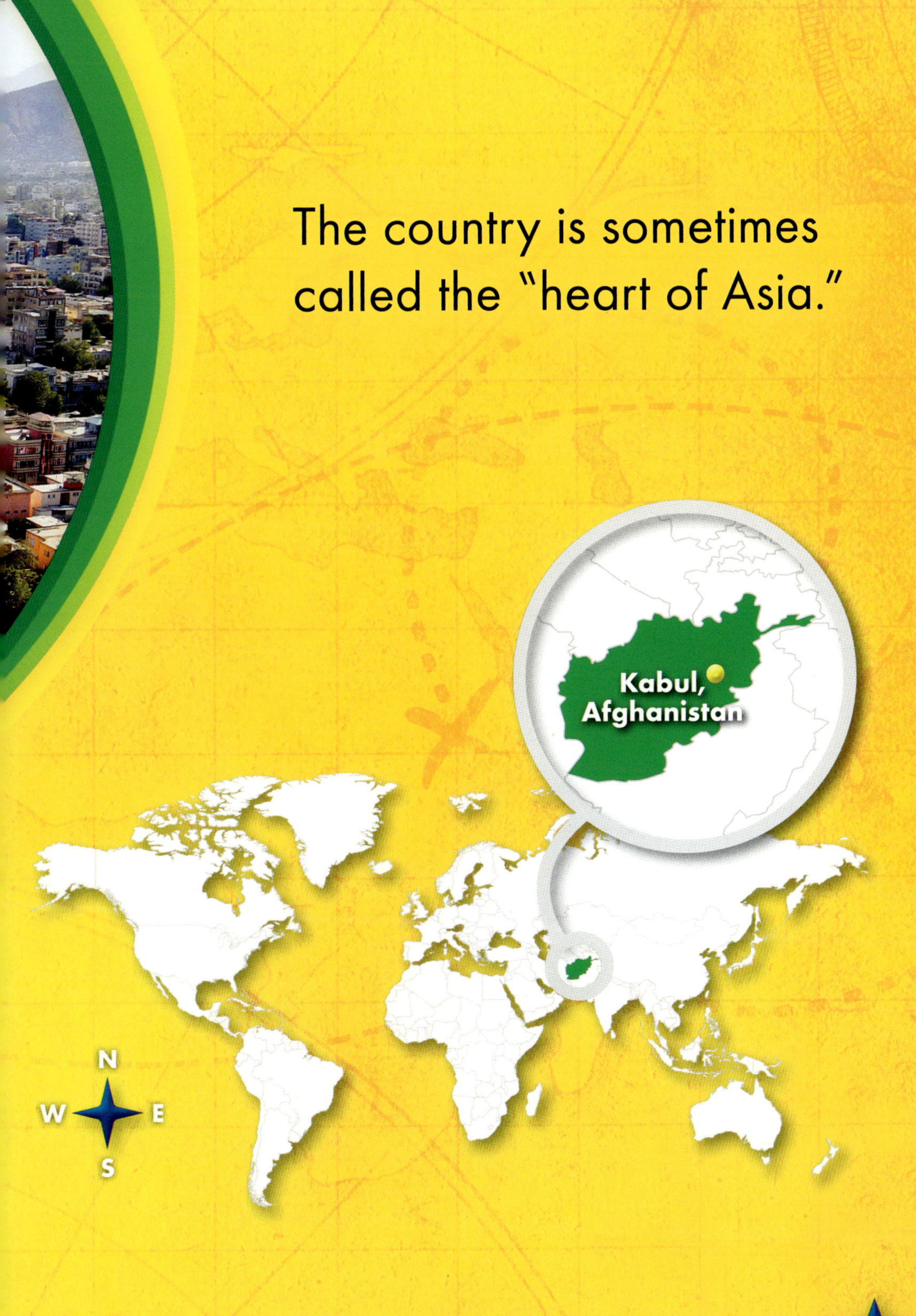

Land and Animals

Mountains cover most of Afghanistan. The Hindu Kush is the main mountain **range**.

Deserts fill the southwest. **Plains** lie in the north.

plains

Mount Noshaq

Size: 24,580 feet (7,492 meters) tall
Famous For: Afghanistan's tallest mountain

Most of Afghanistan is dry. Summers are hot and winters are cold.

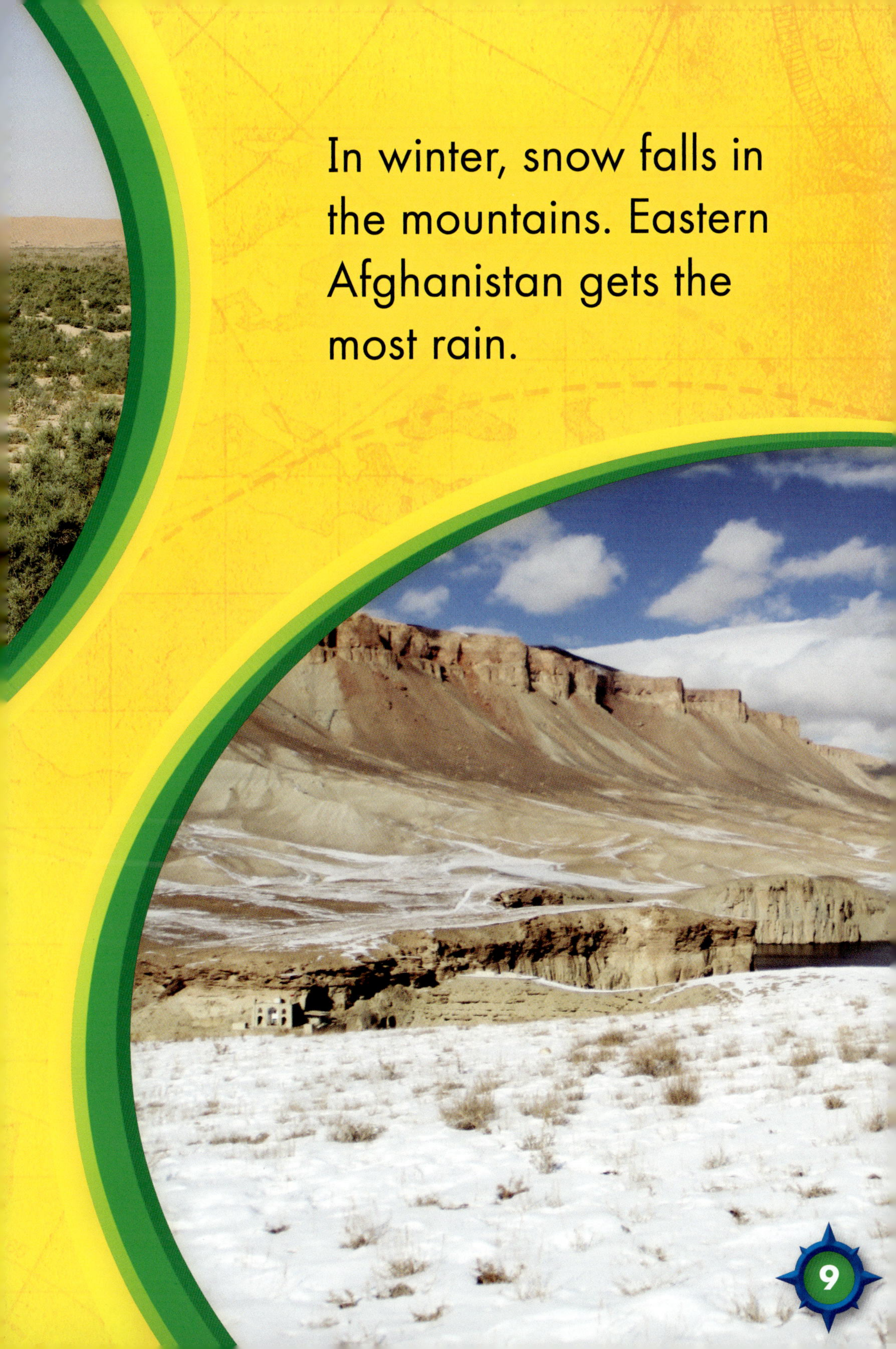

In winter, snow falls in the mountains. Eastern Afghanistan gets the most rain.

Markhor live in the mountains. Snow leopards hunt nearby. Flying squirrels **glide** between trees.

Animals of Afghanistan

snow leopard

red giant flying squirrel

Central Asian cobra

golden eagle

In the desert, cobras eat small animals. Golden eagles fly across the country.

Life in Afghanistan

There are many **ethnic** groups in Afghanistan. Most people speak Dari or Pashto.

Many Afghans live in the country's valleys. They grow crops. They keep **herds** of animals.

English: Hello
Dari: Salam
(sah-LAHM)
Pashto: Salam
(sah-LAHM)

Muslims

flying kites

Almost all Afghans are **Muslims**. They are deeply **religious**.

Many Afghans fly kites. *Buzkashī* is a popular sport. It is played on horseback!

buzkashī

Kabuli pulao is a favorite dish. It has meat, raisins, and carrots. *Bolani* is stuffed flatbread.

Chapli kebab is a spiced meat patty.
Sheer pira is a sweet fudge.

Afghans **celebrate** *Nowruz* in spring. It is the Afghan New Year.

Nowruz

August 19 is **Independence** Day. People listen to speeches and dance together. Afghans are proud of their independence!

Afghanistan Facts

Size:
251,827 square miles
(652,230 square kilometers)

Population:
40,121,552 (2024)

National Holiday:
Independence Day (August 19)

Main Languages:
Dari, Pashto

Capital City:
Kabul

Famous Face

Name: Aryana Sayeed

Famous For: Afghan pop singer and women's rights advocate

Religions

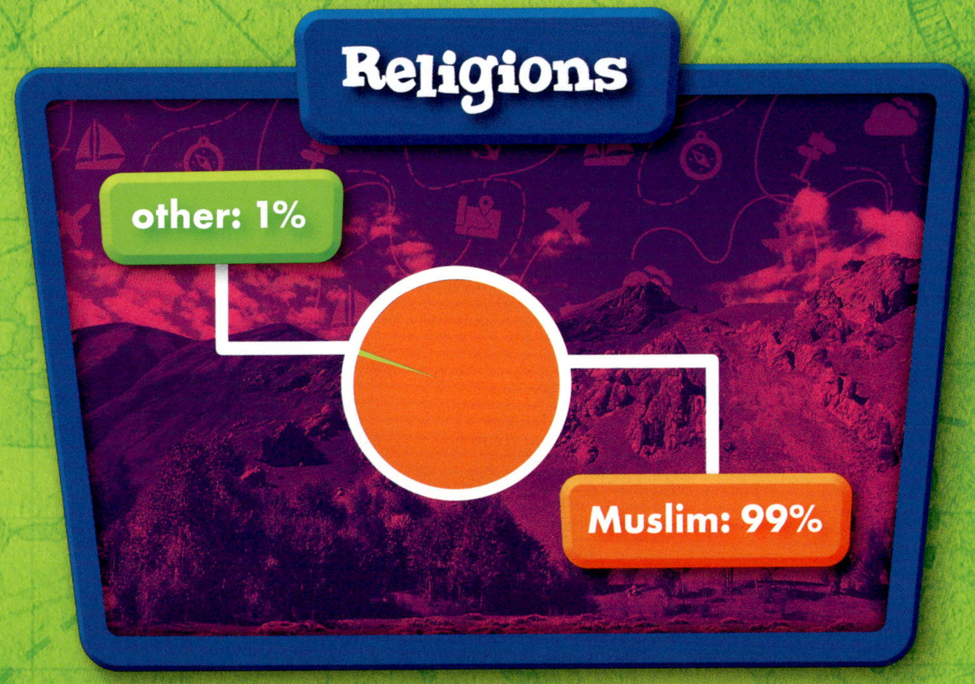

Top Landmarks

Bagh-e Babur

Herat Citadel

Minaret of Jam

Glossary

celebrate—to do something special or fun for an event, occasion, or holiday

deserts—dry lands with few plants and little rainfall

ethnic—related to races or large groups of people who share things such as customs, religion, and language

glide—to fly through the air smoothly without flapping wings

herds—groups of animals that live and travel together

independence—related to freedom from being under control of someone or something

landlocked—enclosed or nearly enclosed by land

Muslims—people of the Islamic faith; Muslims follow the teachings of the Prophet Muhammad as told to him from Allah.

plains—areas of flat land with few trees

range—a group of mountains

religious—having to do with a certain faith

To Learn More

AT THE LIBRARY

Mattern, Joanne, and Sophie Washburne. *Afghanistan*. Buffalo, N.Y.: Cavendish Square Publishing, 2024.

Orr, Nicole K. *Awesome Animals of Asia: The Continent and Its Creatures Great and Small*. Mount Joy, Pa.: Curious Fox Books, 2024.

Peterson, Christy. *Welcome to Afghanistan with Sesame Street*. Minneapolis, Minn.: Lerner Publications, 2022.

ON THE WEB

FACTSURFER

Factsurfer.com gives you a safe, fun way to find more information.

1. Go to www.factsurfer.com.
2. Enter "Afghanistan" into the search box and click 🔍.
3. Select your book cover to see a list of related content.

Index

The images in this book are reproduced through the courtesy of: robertharding/ Alamy Stock Photo, front cover, p. 12; GrafixersINC, p. 3; Nasir Ahmad Salehi, p. 4; The Washington Post/ Contributor/ Getty Images, p. 6; tracingtea, pp. 6-7; Priakhin Mikhail/ Alamy Stock Photo, p. 8; Qader jebran talash, p. 9; BearFotos, p. 10; jindrich_pavelka, p. 11 (snow leopard); Scott Canning, p. 11 (red giant flying squirrel); Omid Mozaffari/ Wikipedia, p. 11 (Central Asian cobra); Gerdzhikov, p. 11 (golden eagle); Waheedullah Jahesh, pp. 12-13; US Army Photo/ Alamy Stock Photo, p. 14 (top); U.S. Department of Defense Current Photos/ Wikipedia, p. 14 (bottom); Xinhua/ Alamy Stock Photo, p. 15; Didebashvili.GEO, p. 16 (Kabuli pulao); Sergii Koval, p. 16 (bolani); highviews, p. 16 (chapli kebab); PI, p. 16 (sheer pira); Jono Photography, p. 17; Imago/ Alamy Stock Photo, pp. 18-19; Manny Carabel/ Contributor/ Getty Images, p. 20; RobNaw, p. 21 (Bagh-e Babur); Sirio Carnevalino, pp. 21 (Herat Citadel, Minaret of Jam); photomaster, p. 22.